"A faithful friend is the
medicine of life."
— Ecclesiasticus 6:16.

Poetry   # Contents

p28

Country Calendar

Thinkstockphotos.

From The Manse Window

p158

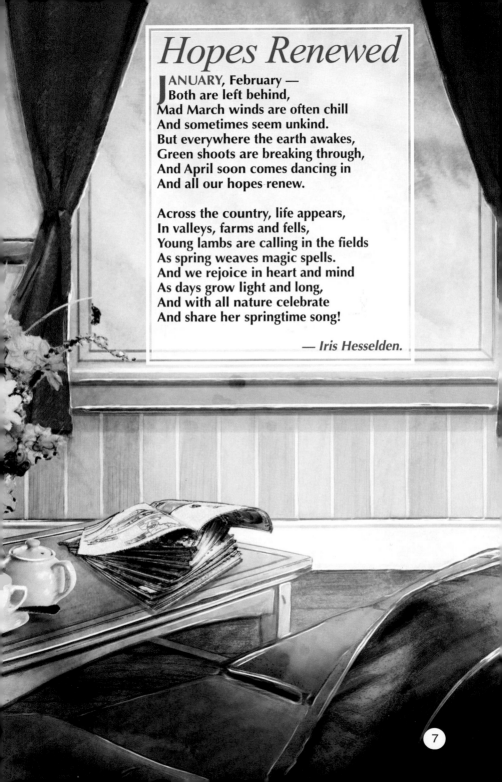

Hopes Renewed

JANUARY, February —
Both are left behind,
Mad March winds are often chill
And sometimes seem unkind.
But everywhere the earth awakes,
Green shoots are breaking through,
And April soon comes dancing in
And all our hopes renew.

Across the country, life appears,
In valleys, farms and fells,
Young lambs are calling in the fields
As spring weaves magic spells.
And we rejoice in heart and mind
As days grow light and long,
And with all nature celebrate
And share her springtime song!

— *Iris Hesselden.*

Poised

NOW, on the very edge of spring,
Time trembles, like a raindrop poised,
Suspended on a leafless bough,
To fall, to fall to earth.

And all at once the moment comes.
Spring's here! A splash of colour spreads,
White pools of snowdrops, nodding heads,
A wave of scillas, blue and bright,
A yellow swell of aconite,
Sweet celandines in golden swirl,
Sprays of catkins dip and whirl,
The tide of spring engulfs the earth,
A flood of joy in life's rebirth.

— *Maggie Ingall.*

Wishes

I **WISH** you the comfort of silence
As the noisy world goes by,
And quiet peace to touch your life
As gently as a sigh.
I wish you the joy of the morning
As the sky is filled with light,
With tranquil thoughts as daytime ends
And stars shine in the night.

I wish you a rainbow after storms
And a soft wind from the sea,
With small wildflowers round your path,
Which others may not see.
I wish you the gift of caring friends
Who will always lend a hand,
They help to keep your dreams alive
And always understand.

I wish you the beauty of nature,
The wonder of all you can see,
With love growing stronger around you,
And all that tomorrow can be.

— *Iris Hesselden.*

A Springtime Song

IN the dreary, dark heart of the winter,
The sun shows a sliver of light,
But each day, with lengthening minutes,
Pushes back the kingdom of night.

With rising hope the world will awaken
Each day to an earlier morn,
And the sun can be seen at breakfast time,
And alarm clocks will sound after dawn.

Folks will return to their gardens,
With the sun setting later each day,
They'll mow their lawns when they get
   home from work,
And children will go out to play.

The earth's moving in its orbit,
The world's singing a springtime song,
The days of darkness are numbered,
The hours of sunshine are long!

— Antony Burr.

from the Manse Window

Rural Ways

PERHAPS it is because they work so much outdoors and are frequently exposed to the icy winds of winter that country folk find such great joy in their anticipation of the coming of spring! I have a warm regard for country ways, especially the manner in which folk greet total strangers when they meet.

I was never actually a country dweller, but I did work for several years on a farm. It happened, without intending it, that I took my first steps to becoming a country lad. Facing the prospect of the long school holidays, I resolved to earn some money by picking fruit. So, early one morning, I caught a bus out to a farm where I knew they grew fruit.

From the number of youngsters already present I realised immediately, as I was curtly informed, that they had no need of any help from me! A little disappointed, I made my way to another fruit farm a mile away, but I had no better success there, either!

Nevertheless, with the whole morning stretching before me, I was reluctant to give up and go home. So I followed a country road along leafy lanes, up hill and down dale, going from farm to farm knocking on doors, looking for work.

Though sympathetic, people had no work to offer me. The best they could do was to point me in the direction of the next farm. I must have trudged the best part of eight miles that morning, eventually arriving at a smallholding at the end of a rough track at Summerston in the Kelvin valley.

I was greeted by the loud barking of half a dozen dogs which, to my immense relief, were enclosed in a paddock. I stood at the green door of this little farmhouse and knocked nervously. The lady who opened it looked down on me with kindly amusement and called her husband, Jack. He, too, looked down on me and asked what I wanted.

"I am looking for a job," I said uncertainly, adding lamely, "I could pick fruit."

"How old are you?" he enquired.

I drew myself right up to my full four foot and two inches and answered, "Fourteen".

To my great surprise, he took me on. At six old pence an hour. Twenty shillings for a whole week! To penniless me, who had never had a paid job in my life, it was money for old rope!

I discovered that the farm was really a breeding kennel for gun dogs — Labradors, setters and spaniels. However, with the outbreak of war, the Ministry of Agriculture was not

Continued on page 16.

By Arthur J. Brown B.D.

A Country Calendar For ...
Spring

● February 12, 13 and 14 are traditionally said to be "borrowed" from January – if they're stormy, the rest of the year will enjoy good weather, but if those days are fine, the whole year will be foul. Here's hoping for a stormy Valentine's Day!

Thinkstockphotos.

Thinkstockphotos.

● Snowdrops are beautiful and also symbolic of hope. It's said that when Adam and Eve were thrown out of Eden, and Eve was on the verge of giving up hope that the cold winters would ever end, an angel appeared and transformed some of the snowflakes into snowdrops, showing that winters do, eventually, give way to spring.

from the Manse Window

Continued from page 14.

prepared to allow all those acres to be given over to dogs.

My transition to becoming a country lad absorbing rural ways began slowly but continued steadily. Before long I found myself in a completely new world of dogs, pigs and poultry, crops and fruit-picking. We had a small copse of apple trees, and from our blackcurrant bushes I acquired the discipline of picking every single berry from one bush before going on to the next. But not so with strawberries. With strawberries I was allowed to eat more than I gathered!

I was also responsible for cooking

16

● Candlemas Day, on February 2, is the Christian festival of lights. It falls at the mid-point of winter, halfway between the shortest day and the spring equinox, and is the day, traditionally, when all the candles for the coming year were brought into church to be blessed.

Thinkstockphotos.

● Mothering Sunday is also known as Simnel Sunday, and always falls on the third Sunday before Easter. It is thought that simnel cakes were first made by girls in service to take home to their mothers on Mothering Sunday, and the cake's topping of eleven balls of marzipan represents Jesus's eleven faithful disciples – Judas is omitted.

FACT – Both the Romans and the Celts regarded February as the start of spring, and the word *februa* means cleansing or purification – reflecting the origin of a good spring-clean!

half a ton of potatoes for the pigs, twice daily, in a huge boiler at the back of the pig house. Another daily task was breaking a large binful of bread which, soaked with meat or fish stock, was used for feeding the dogs.

We also had a retired horse called Mary, who pulled the plough as the occasion arose. Mary had spent her working life pulling a milk cart in Edinburgh, and had been trained to stop every twenty yards or so at each tenement entry to allow the milkman to dash up the stairs with his bottles. Her training was truly reflected in her spasmodic ploughing!

Beyond the farm was a gently sloping meadow where a neighbouring farmer grazed his cows and sheep. Behind this meadow was

Continued on page 18.

from the Manse Window

Continued from page 17.

a lane winding through the woods to a five-bar wooden gate leading to a road, which I soon found was a convenient shortcut home.

The longer I worked on the farm, the richer grew my appreciation of the countryside. I loved the beauty of the ever-changing seasons. That particular summer proved to be one of long warm days and balmy evenings that seemed to last for ever. They were days to be enjoyed.

With all the demanding things that had to be done on a livestock farm, it was easy to lose all sense of time and work on, blissfully unaware that the evening had gone. As soon as I was finished, I would grab my coat and hurry over the meadow and down the woodland track to catch my bus, which, more often than not, I missed. This left me with an extra two-mile walk before reaching home. In the end I just had to put down sufficient deposit on a bicycle, and buses ceased to matter!

The pleasant days of summer drifted into autumn and our cornfields were ready for harvest and reaping. Mary, of course, was reluctantly involved and we piled the sheaves up in the old-fashioned manner in what we called "stooks" to let them dry out in the sunshine.

Harvest Thanksgiving seemed more real to me now that I was involved in it so closely. Going to church remained an important part of my young life, and my country experience not only prepared me in later years to understand the people in my country congregations, of which I had several, but to appreciate the very fact that those people were in church at all. Farming is a demanding seven-days-a-week occupation and the farming families have to make a special effort to attend church.

EVEN in the city, I had always been aware of the beauty of autumn, but the golden tints of the copper beeches interspersed with the continuing dark green of spruce and larches were something I could only appreciate fully in a country setting.

The departure of flocks of migratory birds along with putting our clocks back at the end of October was a sure and certain herald of the approaching bleak days of winter.

With the coming of colder winds I began to wonder how I might manage to work outdoors over the approaching winter during months of ice and snow. There are few places to shelter when working on an open farmyard, and the best anyone can do is to wrap up warm. That winter proved to be particularly long and bitter with snowdrifts on the track through the woods, and to all of us, not least me, spring seemed painfully reluctant to come.

But winter had its own attractions. The quagmire created by autumn rains froze into solid earth and we no longer squelched through mud. Also, as the farm had no electricity and relied on paraffin lamps for its lighting, our working was curtailed to the hours of daylight and I was able to set off for home around five o'clock!

Throughout December, the weather

proved gloomy and dismal followed by four weeks of equally miserable intermittent rain. For country people, more so than city dwellers who take street-lighting for granted, the anticipation of spring is like waiting through a long dark night for the coming of the dawn.

One early and welcome indication of the return of spring is the arrival of the snowdrops, followed by the crocuses. Then almost, it seems, overnight, the barren branches of trees and hedgerows burst into a flurry of green of many hues. At the same time, the meadows are transformed from straw-coloured drabness into lush grass. Before long our copse of apple trees is bedecked with white blossom, as are our fruit bushes.

Golden daffodils appear in odd corners and periodically alongside the roadways, and later on the woodlands are carpeted with bluebells. The sheep come back to the meadow with their skipping lambs, as do the cows with their delightful long-legged calves.

Another sign of spring is the return of the migrant birds as they come sweeping in flocks across the valley, back to their former haunts and their old nests. Putting our clocks forward in March abruptly restores the lighter evenings and raises the curtain to the ultimate return of spring. The whole world becomes brighter, with an immediate promise of warmer days and spring sunshine providing pastoral scenes worthy of a chocolate box.

Suddenly, at long last, the waiting is over and spring has arrived in all its beauty and fullness, and in my heart I can sing the words of the familiar well-loved May Day carol.

"The glory of the spring how sweet, the newborn life how glad!

What joy the happy earth to greet in new, bright raiment clad." ●

Willie Shand.

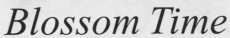

Blossom Time

BLOSSOM time is here once more,
As laden boughs to heaven soar,
With every shade and tint and hue,
Each shining petal, bright and new.
Hawthorn, sorbus – creamy white,
And elderberry, shining bright.
Rhododendrons all aglow,
From palest pink to indigo.
Cherry, apple, almond, pear,
Put on a show beyond compare.
Wisteria tassels, lilac's haze,
Vie with laburnum's golden blaze.
It seems that they all coincide,
To colour town and countryside.
Small wonder that our spirits sing
When blossom blooms again in spring.

— *Brian H. Gent.*

The Heralds

So brave, so bold, the daffodils,
Who pay no heed to winter chills,
But bloom defiant, sharp and bright
To fill bleak days with hope and light,
And lift the hearts of all who glance
Upon their wild and windswept dance,
Their trumpets raised in gallant shout
To blast the last of winter out.
Such happiness their flowers bring,
While heralding the days of spring!

— *Maggie Ingall.*

23

Mother's Day

YOU are truly wonderful,
You are quite unique,
And if I climbed a mountain
And reached the highest peak,
I'd never find an equal
To match those caring smiles,
And just to see your loving face
I'd walk a million miles.
Although I know, when I was young,
I didn't always see
All the myriad little things
You planned and did for me;
But now that I am older
I can look back and know
The many, many reasons
That make me love you so.
That's why at this special time
I'd simply like to say,
I hope you have the very best
And happiest Mother's Day!

— *Brian H. Gent.*

Timeless Spell

THE mountains wear their shawls of snow,
But melting waters sing
And tumble to the glens below
To welcome radiant spring.

The joyous chorus of the birds
Awakens us at dawn,
To tell us, without need of words,
That beauty is reborn.

The buds are bursting on the trees,
New lambs bleat on the brae,
Blue islands set in turquoise seas
Their ageless charms display.

Now spring walks barefoot on the hills
Through iridescent showers.
She gilds dark pools and mountain rills
And wakes the moorland flowers.

For her our sweetest songs are sung,
Our poets know her well,
And winter-weary hearts grow young
Beneath her timeless spell.

— *Brenda G. Macrow.*

The Bright Side

IN life there is always a bright side
Should things look forbiddingly grim;
Though mud mars the scene at the ebb tide
With the high tide, the sea flows back in.

When clouds in the grey skies are bursting,
Till torrents of rain cascade down.
Before long, the sun will shine brightly
And a rainbow will arch o'er our town.

After chilling winds bite us in winter,
And a cold, nippy air strikes our face,
Spring's warmth will envelop the bare land
Which her carpet of flowers will embrace.

Should we enter a tunnel incessant
With darkness and gloom end to end,
As blindly we worm our way through it,
A chink of light creeps round the bend.

So even though grim seems the outlook,
A bright side awaits to appear.
Just give it a chance to take over
And put the dark side to the rear.

— *Joan Zambelli.*

29

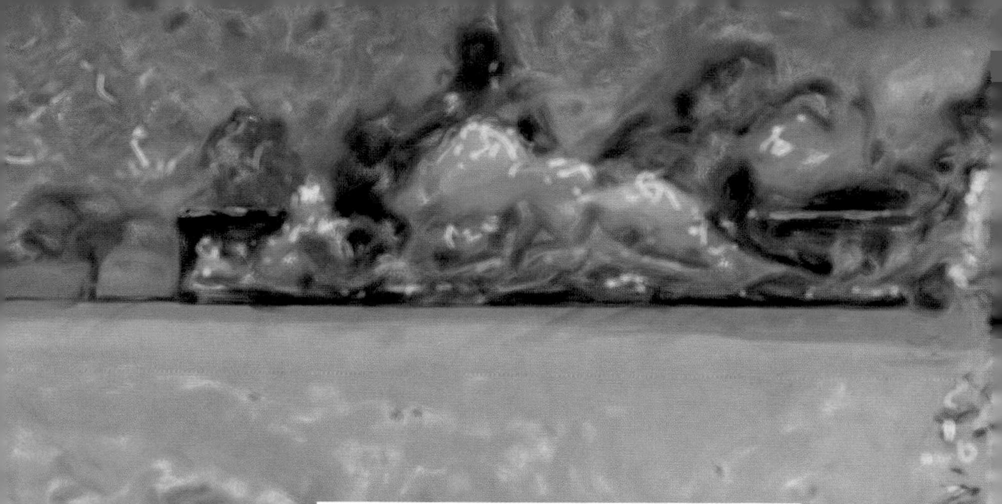

Laburnum

FROM spring when you awaken,
Until your petals fall,
You remind me of mimosa,
The loveliest flower of all.
From beaches in far Cyprus
Across the sunlit seas,
Your blossom brings me memories
Of long-lost magic trees.

Once long ago, when Mother lived
In that warm, sunny clime,
She told me of her homeland
And the history that was mine.
She told me of the avenues
That set the shore aflame,
All along the seashore road
That come each year again.

Because mimosa often dies
Outside in this cold land,
To laburnum I must say,
"I hope you understand."
But the winds that stir your blossom
Seem to whisper where you stand,
"You won't be disappointed,
I'm the fairest in this land"!

— *Dawn Lawrence.*

A Clean Sweep

No putting off, today's the day,
The time has come to sweep away
Cobwebs, clutter, all that stuff,
My home's a mess, I've had enough.

I'll sweep clean with a brand-new broom,
Bring space and light to every room.
I'm eager, yes, I'm mustard keen,
So watch out house, it's your spring clean!

For I once read in a magazine
That to declutter and spring clean
And do it properly, you ought,
Not just throw out but also sort!

A pile for charity, yes, I should
Be grateful I can do some good,
A pile that, frankly, there's no doubt
Is only fit to be thrown out!

Mission accomplished! Now I smile
And smugly contemplate each pile.
Job well done, so I will take
Time out and have a coffee break.

But then I feel my spirits drop,
The stuff meant for the charity shop,
Well, surely there are things I'll need,
Those tops to wear, those books to read . . .

Once more I feel my spirits dip
For in the pile aimed for the tip
Are things — I must own up to this —
That I know I would sorely miss!

Perhaps I'll save a thing or two,
For what's the point of buying new?
The two piles have become a heap,
That's twice as big, labelled *To Keep*!

— *Deborah Mercer.*

33

from the Manse Window

"Peace Be With You"

HAVE you ever wondered why some Easter cards carry the greeting "Easter Peace"? Why an event so explosive and life-changing should be linked with the word peace? Yet the first words the Risen Jesus spoke to his disciples were words of peace. On the evening of that first day of the week, when the disciples were fearfully gathered together, Jesus came and stood among them and said, "Peace be with you."

I've always imagined that greeting to be a kind of holy salutation, but I wonder now whether it was more along the lines of "Don't panic!" After all, deceased men don't tend to rise and suddenly appear!

The disciples were terrified: they thought they were seeing a ghost. But there were so many other emotions swirling around, too. They were cowering behind locked doors, fearing the might of Rome and the religious authorities. They knew now that they were never going to win, that they'd been deluded after three years of fellowship and miracles and challenging the way things were.

John had stood at the foot of the cross and watched their leader die. They were afraid that the same fate awaited them. No doubt they were planning to lie low for a while before escaping from the city and going back to their old anonymous lives. This whole experience would just be a strange interlude they might tell stories about to their grandchildren one day.

They were also dealing with guilt and an awareness of their shortcomings — they'd run away, deserted their leader. Peter had even denied him, after all his boasting of how he would die with Jesus. They were a bunch of failures who hadn't even been able to sense that Judas was up to something. I wonder how many arguments they had amongst themselves over that, blaming each other. How they must have berated themselves for not being able to stop him.

And to crown it all there were the strange things that had happened that morning — the story the women brought them, Peter and John discovering the empty tomb. You know what it's like when you're emotionally overloaded and you can't think straight any more — it often leads to a thumping headache and a desire to be able to switch off and not have

Continued on page 36.

By the Rev. Susan Sarapuk.

A Country Calendar For . . .
Spring

Thinkstockphotos.

● Keep an eye on oak trees, which provide the perfect breeding ground for a whole range of species of birds, from woodpeckers to warblers, because of the vast numbers of small caterpillars the trees attract – perfect sustenance for parent birds to take back to a hungry brood!

Thinkstockphotos.

● Lent's traditional games are marbles and skipping, which were stopped on the stroke of twelve noon on Good Friday. In some places, the day was actually called Marble Day or Long Rope Day.

from the Manse Window

Continued from page 34.

to deal with things. I think the disciples were at that point.

So when Jesus appeared, it's not hard to imagine their absolute terror and confusion.

"Peace be with you." These were the words they needed to hear; peace was what they needed to experience before they could move on.

Isn't that what we want, too? For those caught up in the horrors of war or natural disasters, or a family crisis, or sickness or bereavement — sometimes we just want to be able to switch off for a moment, to be assured that everything is going to be all right.

Thinkstockphotos.

*March hack ham,
Comes in like a lion,
Goes out like a
lamb.*

● Watch out for migrating toads, frogs and newts! Their annual journey to breed back in the lake where they spawned starts in springtime. The rush usually begins on the first warm, rainy, slightly cloudy evening of spring.

● The cuckoo's arrival back in Britain happens in the spring, usually in April. Various dates are called "Cuckoo Day" and some places even hold "Cuckoo Fairs", but an old rhyme tells us that the cuckoo sings from St Tiburtius's Day, on April 14, until St John's Day, on June 24.

Thinkstockphotos.

FACT — The Anglo-Saxon name for April was Eostre monath or Eastremonath, and this is thought to be where the name "Easter" came from.

We know that nobody can wave a magic wand and make it all go away, but what we need is a different perspective, an assurance that there is more to life than what we see, and that ultimately all will be well.

Henry Drummond tells the story of two artists who each painted a picture to illustrate their idea of peace. One painted a scene of a still lake surrounded by mountains. The other painted a thundering waterfall with a fragile birch tree bending over the foam. At the fork of the branch a robin sat in its nest, secure. Most of us would want to identify with the first picture, yet life is more like the second — finding peace and a place to rest in the midst of tumult.

I have no doubt that when Jesus

Continued on page 38.

from the Manse Window

Continued from page 37.

spoke those words of peace and showed them his wounds the disciples were convinced he was real, and everything changed. Bleakness and grief turned to joy and possibility.

Their problems weren't over — in many ways they were just beginning — but that didn't matter. There's a different kind of peace with God. The Apostle Paul calls it "The peace of God that passes all understanding". You can be in the midst of terrible things and yet know that all will be well.

We all want to know what lies ahead of us, from the moment we become aware. Will I get on at school? Will I pass my exams? Will I get a job? Will I meet someone and marry? Will I have children? Will I have a home? Will I have good health? Life is filled with uncertainties.

No-one has a crystal ball and none of us knows how we will cope with difficult times, which come to us all at some stage. Recently I had to go into hospital for the first time ever to have an operation. Yes, I was apprehensive, and even afraid, yet I knew that God was with me.

Peace comes from knowing that, ultimately, things will turn out for good. Peace comes from knowing your place in God's creation so you don't have to look up at the stars at night and wonder, "Who am I?" Peace comes from knowing that you belong, that someone is praying for you. Peace comes from being with Jesus.

The two disciples walking on the road to Emmaus sensed it.

"Were not our hearts burning within us?" they recalled as the stranger who walked alongside them had opened the scriptures to them. As Jesus appeared to these two men and then revealed himself in the breaking of bread as he shared a meal with them before disappearing, all the pain and turmoil, all the sickness of heart was forgotten. They rushed back to Jerusalem to let the rest of the brethren know that all the rumours were true — Jesus was alive.

We might say, "Oh, if only I had been there. If only I could see him." But remember what Jesus said to Thomas, who wasn't there on that occasion and refused to believe the account of his fellow disciples until he'd seen the evidence for himself: "Because you have seen me, you have believed; blessed are those who have not seen and yet have believed."

WE live in an increasingly secular society. One morning close to Easter I was queuing up to buy bread in the local bakery. A customer asked for some hot cross buns.

"Are they special?" the girl who was serving asked. "What does it mean?"

The customer mumbled a "yes", but couldn't give an explanation. So I stepped in and told her that Christians celebrate Jesus dying on the cross on Good Friday.

We seem to be losing touch with our Christian roots. Despite that, people still instinctively feel that there has to be something more, particularly when life can be so hard and unfair for many.

But is it really so different from how

it was at that first Easter? The disciples still had to go out into a hostile world with a message many people didn't want to hear. They would be challenged, often ridiculed, and some of them would ultimately be martyred. They had conviction and the peace of God in their hearts because they'd seen the Risen Lord and knew what was real. The uncertainty, the pain and the doubts had been replaced with the peace of God, which can't really be explained; it needs to be experienced.

Easter reminds us that all is not as it seems on the surface. Even the earth is being renewed at this time of year — a mirror of what is to come in eternity. The ground may be hard, but delicate snowdrops will push through. The mornings are still dark but a blackbird will begin to sing.

In the darkest times, when we feel like utter failures, when it seems that all is lost and that there will never be joy again, Jesus says, "Peace be with you." And we take him at his word. Because of the resurrection everything has changed. ●

Willie Shand.

All At Once

ALL at once the sky is blue,
The days are bright and longer, too.
The trees are slowly turning green
With dainty blossom plainly seen.

The nesting birds are all on the go,
Swooping high and diving low.
Looking for some straw and yarn
To make a nest, both firm and warm.

The bulbs we planted long ago
Have made a most delightful show
Of daffodils, whose golden heads
Light up the garden's flower beds.

The baby lambs cavort and play,
Delighting in this perfect day,
While, far away and out of view,
We hear the sound: *cuckoo, cuckoo.*

And on the lawn so fresh and green
Some daisy heads can now be seen;
These little signs a message bring,
That, all at once, it's spring, it's spring!

— Alice Drury

Easter Days

WHEN frosty winter starts to fade,
We look for signs of spring;
The pussy willow's silver gleam,
Gold catkins as they swing.

Pale primroses upon a bank,
And leaf buds fresh and green;
Bright crocuses and daffodils,
A lovely springtime scene.

We love to watch the merry lambs,
As in the fields they play,
And hear the songbirds' thrilling notes
That greet each sunny day.

And then when Easter Day arrives,
With festive hymns of praise
We celebrate with joyful hearts,
And happy voices raise.

— *Rosemary Bennett.*

43

Bluebell Dreams

BENEATH palm trees, by azure seas, lie the dreams of many folk,
But give me an hour midst the bluebell flowers beneath a canopy of oak.
A shimmering sea of bluebells beneath the towering oak.

Some folk live for music, maybe Bach or rock and roll,
But the silent ringing of the bluebells is the tune that stirs my soul,
Oh, the melodies of the bluebell woods are the music for my soul.

Some folk love their jewellery, their gold and diamonds bright,
But a sapphire gem at the top of a stem is by far a prettier sight,
The sapphire shades of a bluebell are by far a lovelier sight.

Some folk like to travel, there are so many sights to see,
But I've found one that can't be outdone — a bluebell wood for me!
Yes, a bluebell wood in springtime is the place I want to be.

— *Antony Burr.*

Scarecrow

WE are busy in the village
There is no time to play,
For everyone's preparing for
The special Scarecrow Day.
There are scarecrows in the hedgerows,
There's another on the wall,
And two of them parading
Around the Village Hall.
There are scarecrows in old sweaters
And baggy pants and socks,
There are some in sacking aprons
And some in ancient frocks.
Some have pointing fingers,
Some have rolling eyes,
Some of them have heads that move
And take one by surprise.
There is every kind of scarecrow
In every kind of pose,
The only thing they do not do
Is scare away the crows!

— Dorothy Morris.

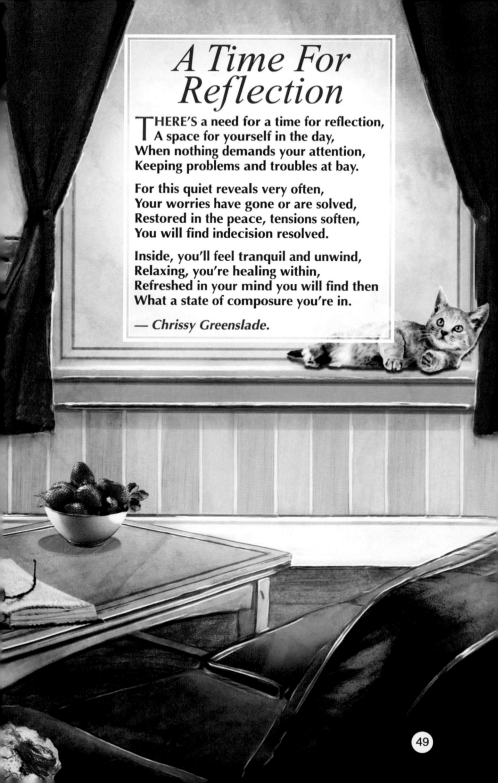

A Time For Reflection

THERE'S a need for a time for reflection,
A space for yourself in the day,
When nothing demands your attention,
Keeping problems and troubles at bay.

For this quiet reveals very often,
Your worries have gone or are solved,
Restored in the peace, tensions soften,
You will find indecision resolved.

Inside, you'll feel tranquil and unwind,
Relaxing, you're healing within,
Refreshed in your mind you will find then
What a state of composure you're in.

— *Chrissy Greenslade.*

Living Flowers

THEY settle on the buddleia
   And I could watch for hours;
Red Admirals and Peacocks
Like living, moving flowers.
With the mildest, faintest tremble,
As though wafted by a breeze,
Their folded wings then open,
And I can gaze at ease
At the richness of their patterns
More exquisite by far
Than the jewels of an emperor,
More glorious than a star.
The crimson of the ruby,
The coal-black of the jet,
The flash of gold in sunshine
All wonderfully set.
They settle on the buddleia
And stay most of the day,
Then later in the twilight
They quickly fly away.

— *Dorothy Morris*

Stepping Stones

DO you remember stepping stones?
It was against the rule,
But still we crossed them when we went
On summer days to school.
The river gurgled out a song
Each lazy afternoon,
When we came chattering home again,
On sunny days in June.
Oh, how I loved those stepping stones
Worn smooth by winter streams,
A makeshift bridge in summer-time,
Warmed through by sunlight's beams.
We used to skip from stone to stone,
To see who jumped the best,
Or pause mid-way to watch the coot
Peep shyly from her nest.
We had to find another path
When winter floods were high,
We could not see the stepping stones
However we might try.
And then we went the long way round,
By muddy road and lane,
And wished so much that we could take
The shortcut once again.

— *Dawn Lawrence.*

A Summer Walk

I LOVE to go out walking in the summer when it's fine
And, as I walk along the paths, the pleasure is all mine.

I pass the little cottages with gardens small and neat,
And smell the scent of lavender and roses, fresh and sweet.
In the distance I can hear some children having fun,
Happy just to be outside and playing in the sun.

A blackbird's singing on a tree and calling to his mate,
And there's a white cat fast asleep beside a garden gate.
And when I reach the countryside the fields look at their best,
The sheep are grazing quietly and the cows are at their rest.

In another field I pass, wild poppies are in bloom,
And as I wander on my way I hum a merry tune,
Beside a tiny babbling brook I find my favourite tree,
Where I can sit and have a rest and eat my picnic tea.

And when I've stayed there for a while, though I wish I could remain,
I have to leave this lovely place and go back home again.

— *Alice Drury.*

from the Manse Window

For Better Or For Worse

AS I look back over my ministry spanning thirty years and more, I recall with untold joy the number of wedding and baptismal services I have had the pleasure of conducting.

It is one of the most precious privileges of the minister to join a man and a woman together in holy matrimony and to invoke the blessing of God on their union. Equally, it is an enormous privilege to baptise a young child and to welcome that child into the family of God, and again, to invoke the blessing of God on the child baptised.

May I just say in passing how wonderful, and very emotional it is to marry one's own children and to baptise one's grandchildren. I have had these unspeakable privileges, too, in my later ministry!

It must be said that of the countless number of persons a minister marries or baptises there are inevitably those which, for one reason or another, stand out!

Let me tell you firstly of the wedding experience of a minister friend. In the process of conducting the marriage service he suddenly had a mental blank and, quite uncharacteristically, he forgot the bride's name!

No matter how hard he tried, he just couldn't bring it to mind, but he did have a brainwave. When he reached the point in the ceremony when he needed to use the bride's name he quietly enquired of her, "In what name do you appear?" To which he was given the sharp response, "In the name of the Father and of the Son and of the Holy Spirit!" The wedding guests were rolling in the aisles!

I, too, have had some hilarious wedding experiences over the years, like the time when I married two seventy-seven-year-olds, George and dear Bessie!

Due to their senior years, they had a bit of difficulty in hearing what I was saying to them, with the result that the ceremony was regularly punctuated and interrupted by the word, "What?"

WHEN it came to signing the wedding schedule, poor George had forgotten his glasses and he entered his name on the line on which the best man should have signed! I'm sure the registrar understood.

On another occasion, I encountered the bridegroom who, when repeating his marriage vows, instead of

Continued on page 58.

**By the Rev. Ian W.F. Hamilton
of Nairn Old Parish Church**

Thinkstockphotos.

A Country Calendar For . . . *Summer*

● Keep your eyes peeled for fallow deer fawns! The result of late autumn's impressive ruts, the single fawns are born in early summer and will spend much of their time alone, hidden in long grass or other vegetation.

Thinkstockphotos.

Thinkstockphotos.

● The Nativity of St John the Baptist falls on midsummer, June 24, and is one of the oldest festivals of the Christian church. It was first listed by the Council of Agde in 506, when it was considered a day of rest punctuated by three Masses: a vigil, at dawn, and at midday.

from the Manse Window

Continued from page 56.

promising to be a "loving, faithful, dutiful husband" assured his bride that he would be to her a "loving, faithful, beautiful husband!"

I once had the pleasure of marrying a fellow minister, who was in fact an Army Chaplain. Accordingly, his correct title was the Reverend Captain. During the ceremony, his bride's garter inadvertently slipped down her leg and it landed on the sanctuary carpet. Nothing daunted, the dashing bridegroom quickly bent down and rescued it — not only did he rescue it,

Mist in May and heat in June Brings all things into tune.

Thinkstockphotos.

Thinkstockphotos.

● From May through to July, but especially during June, villages all over the UK take part in the tradition of well dressing, or well flowering. Starting from the pagan custom of making sacrifice to the gods of wells and springs to ensure a continued supply of water, they are now events for everyone in the area to get involved in!

FACT – June takes its name from the Roman goddess Juno, the goddess of marriage. For this reason, June has historically been looked upon as the best month in which to marry.

but with military precision he slipped it on to his left arm!

The congregation knew that there was something going on up there, especially when the couple and I burst into laughter! I just had to say something!

"The Reverend Captain has just become a Knight of the Garter!" I jocularly announced.

However the *pièce de résistance* must surely be the occasion when the printed orders of service which myself and the wedding party had in our hands up in the chancel became mixed up with the menu for the wedding breakfast, which was to take place afterwards!

Continued on page 60.

from the Manse Window

Continued from page 59.

Thankfully, the guests in the pews had the correct document, but for some reason the wedding party had been given the wrong ones. The service began and when I proceeded to announce the first hymn to be sung, I immediately realised what had happened, as did the bride and groom and bridesmaid and best man when they opened up their "hymnsheets"!

We couldn't contain ourselves and it was obvious to the guests that something was clearly adrift! Once again, I just had to say something.

"The minister has opened the order of service and has landed in the soup — roast tomato soup with smoked ham and juniper berries, in fact!"

ALL of these reminiscences, however, and so many more that I can recall, brought a welcome touch of humanity to these lovely family occasions when their loved ones took those very special vows.

In the course of the wedding services I conduct, I always go on to speak about the meaning of Christian marriage, reminding those concerned that Jesus was once present at a family wedding in a place called Cana in Galilee. Just as he was present there, in that very human situation, God, the Father of all families, is most surely present with them in their human — and sometimes hilarious — situation to rejoice with them, to laugh with them and to bless them as they pledge their lives to one another.

Indeed, I counsel them to ensure that the union taking place at that time is a three-fold union, between themselves, one to another, and between themselves and God, who has brought them each to their very happy and special day.

"If God is invited and enabled to play a central part in your lives and in your home," I conclude, "you may be assured that your marriage will indeed be a thing of beauty and joy for ever."

Baptisms aren't without their "human" moments, too! Well, after all, we are generally dealing with young babies and children who simply aren't aware of what's going on. And it's not uncommon for babies to cry, of course!

To help put them at their ease just before the service begins, I always say to the parents, "Don't worry if the baby brings the house down — it's quite normal!"

Very often, of course, babies in church do let their presence be known in what must for them be a very strange environment. However, I cannot count the number of occasions when howling babies, as they have been passed by their parents to me to baptise them, when I take them into my arms, they suddenly go mute!

"It's the effect I have on them!" I usually say to the congregation, and again a touch of humanity is brought to what can be a rather stressful situation for young parents and their friends in church for the occasion.

* * * *

Not so long ago, however, I had the very opposite kind of baptism experience. The baby was quite perfectly behaved — not so much as a whimper! In fact, she seemed to be enjoying the whole affair as she tried to grasp the minister's collar as he sprinkled her head with water! But it was during the singing of the hymn of blessing, "The Lord bless thee and keep thee" that the child charmed the congregation beyond words.

The organ is situated just beside the baptismal font in our church and the baby was absolutely captivated by the sound of the merry organ and by the animation and dexterity of our organist! No matter how I tried to turn her towards the congregation, the baby — wide-eyed with hands and feet moving in every direction — just refused to be distracted from the musical manoeuvrings before her eyes!

"I think we have an organist in the making here!" I said, immediately after the singing of the blessing.

Who knows what life will hold for all the couples I marry and all the babies I baptise? But one thing is sure, the fact that they have come to the church to seek the blessing of Almighty God on their union or on their little one, they may be certain that in the days and years ahead, God will be ever-present to guide, direct, strengthen and sustain them come what may!

Yes, what a wonderful privilege it is to join couples together in holy matrimony and to baptise and bless their little ones in the name of Almighty God. ●

Thinkstockphotos.

Peaceful Hours

SUMMER days and sunlit mornings
Lift our hearts and minds,
Watching swans serenely gliding
Where the river winds,
Feeling gentle breezes blowing
As the clouds drift by,
Hearing small birds in the tree-tops
And the larks on high.

And so the hours swiftly pass,
The time soon slips away,
Whilst in the west a rosy glow
Announces fading day.
And soon the sky is wonderful
And filled with mauve and gold,
A perfect ending to the day,
A marvel to behold!

— *Iris Hesselden.*

A Perfect Day

A GLORIOUS day in summer,
A village quaint and old,
With gardens full of brilliant flowers,
A picture to behold.
The Morris dancers on the green,
Their ancient skill display,
Their merry music's a delight,
Upon this lovely day.
A pony trap outside the church
Is decked with bands of white,
The bride arrayed in gown of lace,
Commences to alight.
The bells ring out, the parson waits,
The organ starts to play,
As the radiant bride walks down the aisle,
On her perfect wedding day.

— *Rosemary Bennett.*

The Wood

As I walk through
the wood
On summer days
There's a flash of pink
From circling jays,
The dash of a squirrel
Who truly believes
That he's left his cache
Under new-fallen leaves.
The foxgloves stand tall,
The dear cuckoos call,
I love it: the sights,
The sounds, smells and all.

— *Dorothy Morris.*

The Picnic

DAD said, "Let's go for a picnic today,
We'll pack up the hamper and drive far away,
To a forest or beach, a lake or a park,
We'll get there for lunch and stay until dark."

So Mum packed up the hamper with cheese and with ham,
With seed cake and bread rolls and raspberry jam,
Boiled eggs and red apples and iced lemonade,
Pickled onions and salad and biscuits she'd made.

We drove into the country and came to a wood.
Dad parked the car and said, "Here would be good."
The birds were all singing, hidden high in the trees,
While patches of sunlight danced in the breeze.

Mum unpacked from the hamper the rolls of white bread.
"Who's hungry?" she asked. "We all are!" we said.
"That's good!" said Mum, "there's a lot to go round!
Sit yourselves here, on the rug on the ground."

So we filled ourselves up with the cheese and the ham,
Eating platefuls of seed cake and raspberry jam,
We ate all the apples, drank the iced lemonade,
And devoured every one of the biscuits Mum made.

We packed up the plates when the food was all gone,
Then lay on our backs looking up at the sun,
As it shone through the leaves of the trees overhead,
Contentedly drowsy, now we all were well fed.

Then we climbed an old tree and we built our own den,
And everyone hid while I counted to ten,
We chased a few butterflies, played "Robin Hood",
Dad was the sheriff and got caught like he should.

We had to go home when the shadows were long,
In the trees birds were singing their evening song,
Dad drove us home; I fell asleep on the way,
We'd gone out for a picnic; we had a great day.

— *Antony Burr.*

Damson Tree

OUR garden in the summer is a pretty thing to see,
With flower beds and bushes and a lovely damson tree.
And when the fruit is ready and Mum says the time is right,
Dad climbs up the ladder and picks all the fruit in sight.

Now it's time for everyone to come to Mummy's aid,
As there's lots of damson jam and damson jelly to be made.
We fetch the scales and sugar and the ancient jelly pan
And the book on preserve-making which was written by our gran.

And then we all get busy for there's lots to do, you see,
And we help our busy mummy, sisters Jane and Sue and me.
The fruit is washed and weighed and put into the jelly pan
According to the method carried out by clever Gran.

And when the jam is ready it is put aside to cool,
And Mummy says the time has come to make some damson fool.
And when the fool is ready Mummy says we've still got time
To make some damson chutney, which is a favourite of mine.

Just when we think we're finished, Mummy makes some damson cheese,
And sets aside some lovely fruit which later she can freeze.
By this time we are hungry and we long to have our tea,
So Mummy lays the table just for Jane and Sue and me.

We eat our bread and damson jam and then, to our surprise,
Mum gives us damson trifles and some super damson pies.
And sisters Jane and Sue say that they both agree with me,
That we're really very lucky to possess a damson tree.

— Alice Drury.

Sweet Recall

FROM our special dormer window
In our lodgings by the sea,
A fine view of the harbour
Greets the family and me.
For my brother and my sister,
Me and Mum and Dad,
And seagulls screeching overhead
There's good times to be had.
We'll wander out at half-past nine
As the sky shines azure blue
With spades and flags and buckets
And challenges anew.
And, oh, to feel the lapping waves
Our toes in warm, wet sand,
And digging moats round castles
Brings joy since time began.
And there's a special treasure
Just for me, a large pink shell
Which, when I place it to my ear,
Brings sounds I know so well.
It's my own private phone line,
A message from the sea,
Wishing many magic moments
For my family and me.

— *Dorothy McGregor.*

This Dazzling Day

TODAY I took my camera,
The day had dawned so fine
I didn't want to lose it,
But keep it always mine.
I tried to snap the sunshine,
But I missed its warmth, its glow,
I tried to snap the birdsong,
But birdsong doesn't show.
I tried to catch the essence
Of the lavender and thyme,
The hum of busy insects
Where perfumed roses climb.
But how could just a camera
Secure this dazzling day
To store inside an album
And neatly tuck away?
To capture such perfection
It couldn't even start,
There's just one place to hold it,
And that's within a heart.

— *Maggie Ingall.*

from the Manse Window

"Happy Days Are Here Again"

IT was the summer of 1993 — Friday, July 9, to be precise — approximately 2 p.m. on what was to prove a memorable summer day. The occasion in question was a wedding within St Andrew's Parish Church, Dundee, where I was the minister. This historic Trades' Kirk, opened in 1774, is blessed with a well-tended garden. So much so that it is a frequent and well-deserved award-winner in the annual competition in the city.

More importantly, it provides a most pleasant walk up to the church entrance on a good day, which I used to describe at the beginning of worship as a sort of horticultural introit celebrating God's wonderful gift of nature in all its seasons.

The trouble with Friday, July 9, 1993 was that it was at that moment a terrible day, with torrential hailstones the size of golf balls lashing down! The walk from taxi to church was very much an uphill struggle, both literally and metaphorically, in that weather! Heather, the bride, had arrived well on time at the gates of the church, but due to the severe conditions could venture no further, remaining firmly ensconced within the bridal car.

Well, these July hailstones just kept

hammering down, delaying this summer wedding for more than an hour. The worrying thing at this point was that I had another wedding booked in for a mere hour later. I phoned the next bride's home to suggest that she delay her departure for about an hour. Thankfully, she agreed gracefully!

Then, all of a sudden, a quite amazing thing happened. Just as astonishingly quickly as they had appeared, the hailstones stopped coming down and the sun came out, offering the bride, still waiting in the bridal car, a definite hope of meeting her already arrived husband-to-be, Scott, who was awaiting her in the shelter of a bar handily located just over the road.

What sunshine and what a wedding! It was a very happy day for all, in what eventually turned out to be the warmest of summer sunshine. A peculiar thing that sticks in my memory from that day was the steam rising from the melting hailstones, like a summer mist over our lovely church garden!

In case you were wondering, the second couple that July afternoon were rewarded with a more traditional

Continued on page 78.

By the Rev. Ian Petrie.

A Country Calendar For ... *Summer*

● Lammas Day falls on August 1, and up till the reign of Henry VIII's break away from the Catholic Church was the main harvest celebration and marked the beginning of the harvest season.

Thinkstockphotos.

Thinkstockphotos.

● Every summer, Scotland's capital, Edinburgh, becomes a festival city, with hundreds of events as part of the Book Festival, International Festival, Edinburgh Festival Fringe, Film Festival and the Edinburgh Military Tattoo, amongst others. There's no better place to experience summer in the city!

from the Manse Window

Continued from page 76.

summer wedding, confetti replacing hailstones!

All in all that day was a classic Scottish summer's example of providing a taste of all four seasons in one day — an all too regular feature of our weather! But I love our weather for its variety. Who knows what we are going to wake up to next? Every kind of weather has its advantages and disadvantages, so I try never to complain about it. In fact, I'm actually a fan of the cooler nature of our weather, generally preferring my days

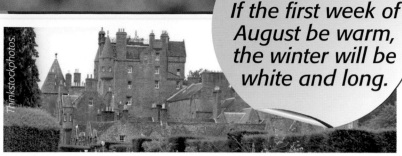

If the first week of August be warm, the winter will be white and long.

● Early September sees one of the east coast of Scotland's biggest family weekends – the Countryside Fair at Glamis Castle. There's a lot to do, from watching some of the horse or craft displays and pony rides to having a go at clay pigeon shooting, archery or fly tying, and dogs (and ferrets!) are welcome along, too. A wonderful way to spend a day, and all in the atmospheric setting of picturesque Glamis Castle, the home of the Strathmore family.

● Keep your eyes peeled for an explosion of beauty in Britain's hedgerows, meadows, sand dunes, shingle pits and in the corners of fields, as a wealth of wild flowers come into bloom, including wild roses, hedge bindweed, rosebay willowherb, orchids and scabious.

FACT – The Anglo-Saxons called August "Weod monath", meaning "Weed Month", because it is the month of the year when weeds and other plants grow most rapidly.

on the cooler side — even in summer!

Home for a few weeks last summer, our son, Gordon, who lives in Tucson, Arizona, commented as we drove through the countryside of Fife via Strathkinness and Peat Inn on our way here to Anstruther, just how colourful it all was.

Now I just love the determined desert scenery in the environs of Tucson, resplendent with amazing cacti gardens. The cacti flower beautifully (and are quite miraculously rooted in the sand) but I understood exactly what he meant. It's something we take so much for granted in this country — its rich colours.

Arguably, the best walk in my life

Continued on page 80.

from the Manse Window

Continued from page 79.

was down the Grand Canyon all the way to the Colorado River. Certainly, the worst walk in my life was all the way up again! The compensation was that it was such a sociable occasion. Well, we would stop and people would walk past and then they would stop and we would walk past again and again and again.

The real highlight for me was the thirteenth-century Indian garden near the foot of the canyon. Simply beautiful, celebrating the promise of nature, which annually never ever lets us down. We must never ever take this promise for granted, pronounced by God after the Flood:

Never again, he promised Noah, will I destroy all living beings as I have done this time. As long as the world exists, there will be a time for planting and a time for harvest. There will always be cold and heat, summer and winter, day and night.

Every season brings the opportunity for promise and fulfilment, even autumn's decreasing light containing the seeds of next year's spring to come.

"HERE Comes Summer", the sole number one by a pop singer named Jerry Keller, was one of the very first 45 rpm records I bought way back when in the summer of 1959, along with "She was Only Sixteen" by Craig Douglas, and "Living Doll" by Cliff Richard at the price of 6s/4d each.

"Here comes summer", Jerry Keller

crooned, "happy days are here again, schools are out, happy days."

We all look forward to summer, don't we? Emerging from the deep darkness of winter, heading into spring as the natural world starts to wake up again, through Easter, my favourite festival, celebrating as it does new life and the life abundant.

Yes, of course, I look forward to summer, too, in my own eccentric way, thoroughly enjoying the lengthening hours of daylight. Once the equinox has passed, though, and the days begin to shorten, I am inevitably reminded of my granny, who — despite suffering the chronic disease of hypochondria — survived well into her nineties.

I well remember visiting her, walking all the way from the west to the east of Arbroath, where she had recently moved to, on June 23, 1965, and what she said to me on that day has very much stuck in my memory.

Making polite conversation, I had suggested what a beautiful day it had turned out to be. Never one to enjoy good news — her glass ever half empty, never half full (except when she was enjoying her sherry) — she replied, "But the nights are drawing in."

Of course, she was technically right, but a mere two days on from the longest day, she seemed almost to be wishing for increasing darkness to overcome decreasing light!

*   *   *   *

For me, summer is all about light, with or without the sunshine. Whatever the summer weather, the light stretches from early in the morning until late in the evening, ever offering the added bonus of warmth.

From as early as the beginning of spring, I am reminded of God's words at the very first day of creation, creating a semblance of order out of chaos.

"Let there be light," he commanded, in what was his first commandment, spoken on the very first day after creating the Universe, when the earth was formless and desolate. Evening passed and morning came — the first day. What a start!

Jesus picked up on that theme when he proclaimed, "I am the light of the world, the light shining in the darkness, which no darkness can extinguish or even comprehend."

That, to me, is the ultimate promise. ●

Thinkstockphotos.

Down At Winkle Bay

ALTHOUGH we live in town, the seaside isn't very far,
And this is very lucky as we haven't got a car.
So when the sun is shining and the school's on holiday,
We catch the country bus and motor down to Winkle Bay.

The journey isn't very far; it's just a mile or two,
And so it isn't long until the sea comes into view.
And when the bus has stopped we all go rushing to the beach,
Where all the things we need for fun are there within our reach.

Mum packs lots of sandwiches and bits of carrot cake,
And little fruity scones, which she's up at dawn to make.
She also packs some apples as they're good for us to eat,
And says she'll buy us ices as a very special treat.

We splash among the shallows and play games upon the sand,
We build enormous castles with a spade and willing hand,
We clamber on the rocks and find some shells which we can keep,
And fish in all the rock pools where the water isn't deep.

We eat our lovely sandwiches, and drink hot cups of tea,
And eat the cake and scones which are as good as they can be,
And as the time is passing and we've had a lovely day,
We pack up all the picnic things and homeward make our way.

And, back at home we sleepy children fall asleep and dream,
Of day trips to the seaside, sandwiches and more ice-cream.

— *Alice Drury.*

83

Timeless Hours

WE walked in meadows deep in buttercups
And hand in hand smiled in delighted glee,
For there were trees, birdsong and insect hum
And nature filled our day with gaiety.

We picnicked dreaming, drowsy with summer heat,
As timeless hours sped by on silent wings.
We bared our feet and cooled them in the stream
And laughed and loved and whispered secret things.

As skimming swallows shared our well-loved place,
Soft breezes swayed the peacock butterfly,
We vowed we would one day come back again,
For this was just farewell and not goodbye.

— *Chrissy Greenslade.*

Waiting For Summer

OH, who has seen the summer?
Wherever did she go?
I've hung on here for ages
Yet still she doesn't show.
I thought I glimpsed her briefly,
In April, then in May,
In June I'm sure I saw her —
But then she went away.
And now the days are passing
And autumn waits her cue.
Oh, summer, we're all waiting,
But where on earth are you?

— *Maggie Ingall.*

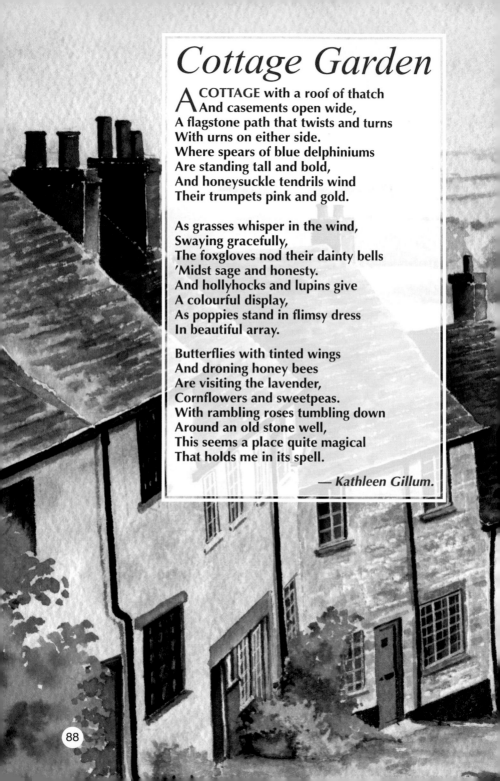

Cottage Garden

A COTTAGE with a roof of thatch
And casements open wide,
A flagstone path that twists and turns
With urns on either side.
Where spears of blue delphiniums
Are standing tall and bold,
And honeysuckle tendrils wind
Their trumpets pink and gold.

As grasses whisper in the wind,
Swaying gracefully,
The foxgloves nod their dainty bells
'Midst sage and honesty.
And hollyhocks and lupins give
A colourful display,
As poppies stand in flimsy dress
In beautiful array.

Butterflies with tinted wings
And droning honey bees
Are visiting the lavender,
Cornflowers and sweetpeas.
With rambling roses tumbling down
Around an old stone well,
This seems a place quite magical
That holds me in its spell.

— *Kathleen Gillum.*

I love
my
Grandma

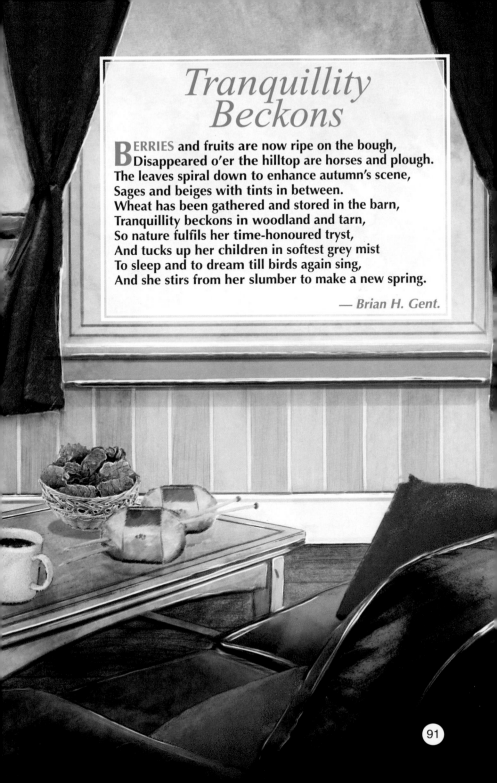

Tranquillity Beckons

BERRIES and fruits are now ripe on the bough,
Disappeared o'er the hilltop are horses and plough.
The leaves spiral down to enhance autumn's scene,
Sages and beiges with tints in between.
Wheat has been gathered and stored in the barn,
Tranquillity beckons in woodland and tarn,
So nature fulfils her time-honoured tryst,
And tucks up her children in softest grey mist
To sleep and to dream till birds again sing,
And she stirs from her slumber to make a new spring.

— *Brian H. Gent.*

Once Again

ONCE again the turn of summer
Yields the first autumnal mist,
And the golden harvest gathered
With the ripened fruits, sun-kissed.

Once again the seasons mellow
And the gifts of God to man,
Through the tending of earth's bounty,
Stay unchanged since time began.

Look upon the fruit of orchard,
Apple, plum and golden pear,
See the vegetables and flowers
All matured through loving care.

From the sunshine's benediction
And the gentle rains of night,
Till the precious dawn is breaking
And the earth awakes to light.

— Elizabeth Gozney.

Harvest Prayer

WE thank you for the harvest, Lord,
   The bounty of your hand.
For every season of the year
Which touches all the land.
For fruit and flowers, trees and plants,
The miracle of seeds,
For food and comfort through the months
Providing for our needs.

We thank you for the love we share,
The harvest of the heart,
For all the precious gifts of life
Your hope and joy impart.
We pray for those less fortunate
Who suffer every day,
Be with them on their journey, Lord,
And help them find their way.

And now, once more, we thank you, Lord,
For blessings great and small,
But, most of all, your endless love,
The greatest gift of all.

— Iris Hesselden.

A Smile A Day

AN apple a day keeps the doctor away."
Perhaps that's not quite true.
But here's a thing I recommend —
A smile a day for you.
A gift that's free for everyone
And welcome all the year,
A gift for strangers in the street
Or those you hold most dear.

A smile can touch a lonely heart,
It could be all they need,
And if they want to share with you,
Well, that's success indeed!
But if some people think you're strange
Or simply turn away,
Don't worry, there'll be someone else
To meet along the way.

So as you give away these smiles
You'll find that it's so true,
You feel much better day by day
As they return to you!

— Iris Hesselden.

"Forget Not All His Benefits"

I N my earlier days I had no great affection for the season of autumn. My youthful opinion was that it offered little more than an unwelcome emphasis of the passing of the brightness and warmth of the long summer days, and a too-early warning of the imminent approach of the cold and gloom of the shorter days of winter.

A pastoral visit I made to a more or less housebound member of my first congregation caused me to view autumn in an entirely different light, though.

On my regular visiting list from the very beginning of my ministry in Newmilns West Church in Ayrshire's Irvine Valley, Mrs MacIntosh was already in her nineties when I first met her and had been a childless widow for more than thirty years. She had no other family, and lived by herself in an attic room which was reached by a flight of narrow wooden stairs which were quite impossible for her to negotiate unaided.

The consequence was that she was never able to get out of her house except when nearby car-owning friends came and carried her downstairs to take her on an outing.

On my first visit to her I was briefly deceived into thinking that she had become slightly mentally disorientated owing to her advanced years and her isolation from the outside world.

What happened was that in the course of our conversation she somehow got on to the subject of the famous Scottish missionary explorer, David Livingstone. She started to speak of how she recalled the intense excitement that gripped the whole country when Livingstone returned from his history-making journey across the then still largely unexplored continent of Africa.

"That was a wonderful day," she said as she leaned across to tap me on the knee. "I know you will remember it well," she added.

Since that event had taken place many decades before I was even born, it is perhaps little wonder that her remark made me worry that she had become rather confused.

Very soon, however, I was disabused of that suspicion, as it became abundantly clear as our conversation continued that she was not only in full possession of her faculties but was very sharp mentally.

I realised that in her remark she had

Continued on page 100.

By the Rev. Dr James Martin.

A Country Calendar For ...
Autumn

● It's breeding season for one of Britain's best-loved sea creatures, the grey seal. With the species' largest breeding colonies around the UK's coastline, look out for the very vocal female making a high-pitched hooting noise, or both sexes sleeping vertically in the water, showing only their heads above the waves.

● This is conker season! The fruit of the horse chestnut tree matures and falls in September. Though they get the name "chestnut" from their similarity in appearance to the true, edible chestnut, the fruit is inedible. Children everywhere will agree, though, that they're great fun to play with!

from the Manse Window

Continued from page 99.

simply been telling me that she assumed that I would know about Livingstone's travels, which, indeed, I did.

I very soon discovered, also, that not only was she a person of deep Christian faith but that she possessed a very real philosophical side. It was this later characteristic of hers that led to my transformed view of autumn.

I had been inducted to my charge in the spring and had enjoyed the good weather brought by that season and the following summer. It so happened,

● September 21 – 22 marks the autumn equinox, or the mid-point of the season. This is generally marked, though, on September 29, on Michaelmas — a day of prayer to St Michael the Archangel.

● If you are lucky enough to have a wild cherry tree in your garden, keep a special lookout for bullfinches and warblers at this time of year – they're tempted by the juicy fruit!

Thinkstockphotos.

FACT – The Anglo-Saxons called September Gerst-monath, meaning the "barley month".

however, that I came to visit my old friend on an autumn day which was rather bleak, and I found myself saying to her, "Isn't autumn a depressing season, with summer past and winter soon to come?"

Her reply to that observation not only took me by surprise but also caused me to view autumn for ever afterwards in a totally different – but much more correct – light.

"I can't agree with you, Mr Martin," she said. "There is so much to be said in autumn's favour when you open your mind and heart to what it has to offer. For one thing, just look at the beauty to be seen and enjoyed with all the magnificent colours on display

Continued on page 102.

from the Manse Window

Continued from page 101.

outside at this time of year. You know that I'm not able to get out much to see these things for myself, but my friends came just two days ago to take me for a run in their car. The colours of the leaves on the trees took my breath away. That sight will gladden my heart for days to come."

I was deservedly chastened by this comment and my attitude to the season of autumn was already in the process of changing, but more was to come. She proceeded now to don her philosopher's cloak, and I had, simply, to sit back and listen.

"Not only is there a lot of beauty around in the autumn if we take the opportunity to see it, but autumn is also a very good time of the year, especially for an old housebound lady like me, to delve into the memory basket.

"When God gave us the gift of memory he gave us a truly precious gift, and there is no better time to use it than autumn." At that point she drew my attention to a plaque hanging on her wall which carried, in large letters, the bible text, *Bless the Lord, O my soul, and forget not all his benefits*.

She went on, "I often look at that and think about what it says, especially in the autumn season, when the days are growing shorter and the weather may be getting rougher, and it makes me think of the many blessings God has given me in my passage through life. That helps me a great deal.

"Visitors sometimes say to me that I

must feel very lonely living here all by myself and rarely managing to leave this room. But I never feel lonely because I count my blessings, especially the promise of Jesus to be with me always. Autumn is a very good time to do that."

I left her humble home that day having undergone a remarkable change in my attitude to autumn. That change has remained with me as I think back to that old lady's wise words and remember the biblical injunction on her wall.

Memory, she said to me, is a precious gift from God. That is undoubtedly true and there is no better time of the year than autumn to employ it to the full. It is sad, even tragic, when we forget the good things, the blessings, that have come our way in the past, and instead concentrate our attention on less happy experiences. To do that is a gross misuse of God's gift, and our lives are much the poorer for doing so.

The ministry of memory, properly used, can greatly enrich our lives and even inspire us to face misfortune with courage and victory.

As a boy, I used to spend my school summer holidays with my maternal grandparents at Barjarg in Dumfriesshire, where my grandfather was head gamekeeper on the estate. During one holiday he gave me a little book to read called "Cracks Wi' Robbie Doo", a collection of whimsical tales written by Joseph Laing Waugh, a native of nearby Thornhill.

One of these tales came back to mind as my memory was stirred by receiving that kindly taught lesson in philosophy that afternoon. It told of a woman, well on in years, who kept in the pages of her bible a sprig of "Aipple-ringie" (better known by its proper name of Southernwood), which had been placed there during her teens after it had been given to her by her first sweetheart, as a token of his affection.

Even in her old age, every time she came across it, that sprig made her heart sing with joy as she was reminded of sun-kissed hours long ago.

I do not suppose that many of us, if any, keep a sprig of "Aipple-ringie" in our bibles, but most of us have something similar in our hearts – memories that have the power to lift up our spirits in any kind of weather.

Memories of happy times gone by can exercise a ministry of joy and encouragement in the present – memories of a baptism, perhaps, or a wedding or a birthday or some other particularly glad occasion.

But we may also find help and encouragement in those memories of times of trouble or sorrow when God gave us the strength and the courage to face up to such times and win through them.

Perhaps nothing can be of more assistance to us memory-wise, whatever life's weather may be, than to have written bold in our hearts the words of that bible text on Mrs MacIntosh's wall: *Bless the Lord, O my soul, and forget not all his benefits.* There is no better time to take it out and think of it than when the season of autumn descends upon us, either literally or metaphorically. ●

Willie Shand.

Perfect Plan

A TOUCH of autumn in the air,
The clouds go sailing through the sky,
Brown leaves appearing here and there
And time and tide flow swiftly by.

The scent of wood-smoke on the breeze,
A skein of wild geese overhead.
The evening sun lights fields and trees
And turns the world to pink and red.

All nature has a perfect plan,
A special magic to impart.
So catch the wonder when you can,
And keep September in your heart.

— *Iris Hesselden.*

Autumn Dreams

AS brittle as the corn stalks,
These late autumnal days,
As sharp as leafy wood smoke,
As gold as sunset's rays.
But when the sky grows darker,
And starlight pricks the night,
And through the kitchen window
A haloed moon glows bright,
It's time to close the curtains,
And let the firelight play,
Then dream of long-gone summer,
And Christmas on its way.

— *Maggie Ingall.*

The Fruits Of The Spirit

THE harvest is gathered, the crops brought in,
Give thanks, now, for fruit and for grain.
The bounty of nature, gifts in good measure,
All blessed by the sun and the rain.
The harvest is needed to feed everyone,
To help every day to begin,
But the fruits of the spirit sustain us,
And nourish us daily within.

The harvest of spirit is faith, joy and peace,
With hope for tomorrow today,
With beauty around and love in abundance
And guidance to show us the way.
Rejoice in the harvest and all the earth gives,
Give thanks for the blessings you find,
Reach out to each other with trust and with love,
Share the harvest with all of mankind!

— *Iris Hesselden.* 109

Home Truths

B^E it large or be it small,
Or you are rich or poor,
Just the very thought of it
Can make your spirit soar.
It's a place to put your feet up,
Sit in a chair at ease,
Don your slacks and sweater
And do exactly as you please.
Wander in the garden,
Prune a rose or two,
Or pop into the kitchen
And make your favourite brew.
Potter in the greenhouse,
Thin out those sprouting seeds,
Water your prized marrow
Or hoe persistent weeds.
And when at last the day is done
And warm the fire's glow,
There is one thing for certain
That deep inside you know:
Whether it be near or far,
No matter where you roam,
A special treat is waiting
When, at last, you head for home.

— *Brian H. Gent.*

Russet, Rust And Red

SYCAMORE leaves are turning
To russet, rust and red,
As flowers gently droop their heads
In lane and island bed.
Soon martins, swifts and swallows
Will leave for pastures new,
Where the climate is much warmer
And skies are azure blue.
Spiky conkers hit the ground
For little boys to string,
And those avoiding capture,
Can germinate next spring.
Jack Frost's icy fingers
Will soon open winter's gate,
As little furry creatures
Curl up and hibernate.
The rowan berry clusters
With hips and hawes will vie,
As rolling mists will cover up
The colour of the sky,
So the earth will go to sleep
As lakes become like lead,
And sycamore leaves will tumble down
Russet, rust and red . . .

— *Brian H. Gent.*

Bill's Seat

ALTHOUGH we've never met him —
We only know his name —
We feel so much in tune with him,
For our tastes are the same.

We know Bill loved this coastline,
This was his favourite view,
He loved to rest after his walk
As we and others do.

In pure air filled with perfume
Of gorse, salt and sunbeams,
He'd gaze out to the Isle of Wight;
He'd fulfilled all his dreams.

He'd watch folk swim, go walking,
Enjoy gulls swoop and call,
He'd close his eyes, remembering
In life, he'd done it all.

We always read the words there,
Bill's spirit we still greet,
For we know that he'll be with us
As we share his clifftop seat.

— *Chrissy Greenslade.*

115

Conkers

MY conscience is in tatters and I will not sleep tonight.
No, I should not have done it, it simply wasn't right.
And when their mother finds out, well, I can be sure,
I will become "bad influence" and favourite aunt no more!

But I thought, is it so dreadful? Can it be such a sin?
When he begged, "Please help me, Auntie! I really want to win!"
He was sure that I could help him, and oh, the pride and joy
Of a maiden aunt who's flattered by an eager little boy!

Where's the harm, I told myself, how can it be wrong?
Folk have done the self-same thing for years and decades long!
It isn't really cheating, it's tactics, so to speak,
Just like any sportsman uses, what some would call "technique".

So I took my nephew's conkers and put them in the oven,
And now I have the feeling that my feet are hooves, both cloven.
Oh, those good intentions that pave the road to hell,
But, never mind, next time he asks, I'll vinegar them as well!

— *Deborah Mercer.*

117

The Holy Bread

I HAVE vivid memories of harvest-time among the sleepy summer orchards and hop fields of rural Kent. There was a meadow running down to the main railway line between London and Folkestone, and a tarred wooden fence at the bottom.

Every day we children stood on it to watch the steam engines hurtling past on their way to the coast. Pride of place went to the Golden Arrow, which came by at noon every day, thundering past at eighty miles an hour. If we were lucky, the fireman would give us a wave.

What we liked best of all was watching the shunters at work. The drivers and firemen sent lines of trucks and carriages bumping into stationary wagons with a satisfying crash.

There was an apple orchard nearby and we threw the men fruit in the hope that they would let us ride on the footplate. We pleaded in vain – it was against the regulations.

Tossing those bright red apples over the fence to the waiting railway men when I was six years old is my earliest recollection of the annual harvest. But floating back over the years, there are other happy memories of wartime harvests and rich autumn colours.

We lived in a Victorian vicarage with a large garden. It had many excitements for children, including an ash pit for throwing away burned cinders from the boiler, a woodshed, a summerhouse, a pond with frogs and a bonfire that always seemed to be smouldering. As if that wasn't enough, it contained a wide variety of fruit trees. There was a Victoria plum covered in succulent golden fruit as big as hens' eggs. Also growing there were greengage, cherry, walnut and quince trees. As for apples, there were at least six different kinds, some with cute names such as "Devonshire Quarrenden" and "Beauty of Bath".

The only two trees that did not come up to scratch were the damson and the fig. The damson fruits were small and sour and needed to be cooked in a pie. As for the fig tree, it produced many greeny-purple fruits, but we disliked the taste and texture.

Children in those days were given a daily dose of syrup of figs, and the thought of eating the things from which the foul mixture was made caused us to screw up our faces in disgust.

Harvest-time in the garden was one of the year's highlights. Ladders, apple

Continued on page 120.

By the Rev. David Bryant.

119

A Country Calendar For ... *Autumn*

- October 1 is the start of the old English "pudding season", when puddings both sweet and savoury were made in number. This is thought to originate from the time of year when harvest was finished and farms set about preserving meat rather than having the expense and difficulty of over-wintering large numbers of animals.

- St Francis's feast day falls on October 4. Francis was an Italian Catholic friar and preacher who founded the Franciscan Order and assisted in founding the women's Order of St Clare. He was pronounced a saint by Pope Gregory IX in 1228, two years after his death. He is known as the patron saint of animals and the environment, and is one of the two patron saints of Italy (the other is Catherine of Siena).

from the Manse Window

Continued from page 119.

trays and wickerwork baskets were taken out of the summerhouse and the picking began.

The real excitement lay in climbing. There were always luscious specimens on the greengage and Victoria plum that were out of my father's reach on the ladder, so we would crawl out along the thin limbs, hoping that the branches would bear our weight.

On occasion there was an ominous cracking sound and retreat was instant, but what a sense of victory there was

● St Luke's Day on October 18 often falls in the centre of a short spell of particularly fine weather, and this is known as St Luke's Little Summer. It is a day when girls could have some insight into their future marriage prospects by putting a mixture of spices and honey on their faces and saying the rhyme:

St Luke, St Luke, be kind to me,
In dreams let me my true love see.

● Watch out for the swallows migrating south for the winter! In days gone by, before the birds' travelling habits were understood, people thought they flew into ponds and hibernated at the bottom of them for winter. It's thought this could come from swallows' ability to skim the surface of water to collect insects to eat.

FACT – October brings the Anglo-Saxon Fylleth moon, signalling the beginning of winter. It was also known as Wyn Monath because it was the season of wine-making.

Thinkstockphotos.

when you reached those tantalising fruits and popped one into your mouth!

One of the apple trees was particularly hazardous. It was a variety that the wasps seemed to enjoy, and every time you took hold of a fruit and twisted it off, you risked a fierce buzzing and stab of pain as the insect stung you on the finger. Careful inspection of an apple was essential before eating. Wasps near the mouth were dangerous indeed.

The riskiest climb was the walnut tree. It was a mammoth one with mighty branches, and it was a terror to scramble up. You had to jump up,

Continued on page 122.

from the Manse Window

Continued from page 121.

seize the lowest branch, and try to swing your legs up. We only climbed it when our parents were out of sight, because they considered it to be dangerous. If my mother found out she would stand at the bottom and call out, "Lunch is ready, children." It never failed to bring us down to *terra firma* straight away!

Even in those long-gone days when we were young, we knew that the harvest was something very special for which we should be grateful. This was partly due to our weekly attendance at Sunday school, where we were taught some of Mrs Alexander's "Hymns For Little Children".

Our favourite was "All Things Bright And Beautiful". The teacher played it with great gusto on a tinny piano that had seen better days, and it made us realise that the fruit which we picked, ate and stored with such enjoyment was a gift from God.

Some years later when I was waiting for my National Service call-up papers, I found out how hard farmers work to produce the harvest.

It was 1955 and I was short of money. A friend told me of a contractor who was looking for part-time help on his combine harvesters. I turned up at the office and was signed on as a bag boy, at two shillings and sixpence a week.

It was extremely arduous work. We were driven to a field just as dawn was breaking and as soon as the dew had dried off, the driver would start up with me standing on the rear platform.

There were four bags, filled from chutes, and my task was to tie up the full ones, replace them with empties and throw off the completed sacks at the field corner.

DURING my working life as a parish priest, I took countless harvest festival services in village churches, and it was always encouraging to see the pews full on such occasions. Farmers turned out in their Sunday suits, their families along with them.

The church would be filled with potatoes, marrows, apples, pears, plums, tinned foods, flowers and home-made cakes. On the altar would be a large loaf of bread shaped like a sheaf of corn, and the whole building would be filled with the warm, mellow smell of ripe produce, while the full vases exhibited all the colours of autumn – russet, red, yellow, orange, purple and mauve. There was a real sense of thankfulness that another year's harvest was safely gathered in.

We were all aware that God is to be found at the very heart of the harvest, bringing to the vegetables, plants, trees and flowers germination, fertility, blossom and fruiting. A marrow, a potato, a leek or a grain of wheat – all are a miracle of creation.

The poet John Masefield tells of how Christ is at the centre of the world's harvest in his beautiful poem, "The Everlasting Mercy". His words can be used as a harvest prayer.

O Christ who holds the open gate,
O Christ who drives the furrow straight,
O Christ the plough, O Christ the laughter
Of holy white birds flying after. ●

124

October

THE mornings are foggy
Or silvered with frost,
The days are quite short
Lots of sunlight is lost.
But some afternoons —
What a lovely surprise!
The sun is so strong
That it dazzles our eyes,
And it's pleasant to work
On the garden, to clear
All the surplus from plants
That have thrived there this year,
That gave us such plenty
In produce or fruits,
Some of them need to be
Trimmed to the roots,
And soon it looks tidy,
The hedges are trim,
And the big compost bin
Is filled to its brim,
And though we are tired
We feel very glad
When we think of the year
And the blessings we've had.

— *Dorothy Morris.*

Glorious Land

THE glorious days of autumn,
With leaves of brilliant hue,
When nature's dazzling colours,
Transform our land anew.

She crowns the year with splendour,
Before her winter rest,
And as her final curtain call,
Shows colours at their best.

With yellow, bronze and crimson,
The trees are now arrayed,
As autumn glory once again
Before us is displayed.

— *Rosemary Bennett.*

Pumpkin Pie

WE'VE grown the biggest pumpkin
That you have ever seen,
It's the biggest, roundest pumpkin —
Just right for Hallowe'en.
So we've hollowed out the middle,
And we've made a handsome face,
Two eyes, a nose, a laughing mouth —
Everything in place.
And we've put inside a candle
To make a lantern light
To carry round on Hallowe'en
And give our friends a fright.
And we've played at bobbing apples,
How many did you get?
We've had such a lovely party
And it isn't over yet,
Mummy took the pumpkin centre,
We admit we wondered why,
Then she served it up for supper,
In our favourite — pumpkin pie!

— *Dorothy Morris.*

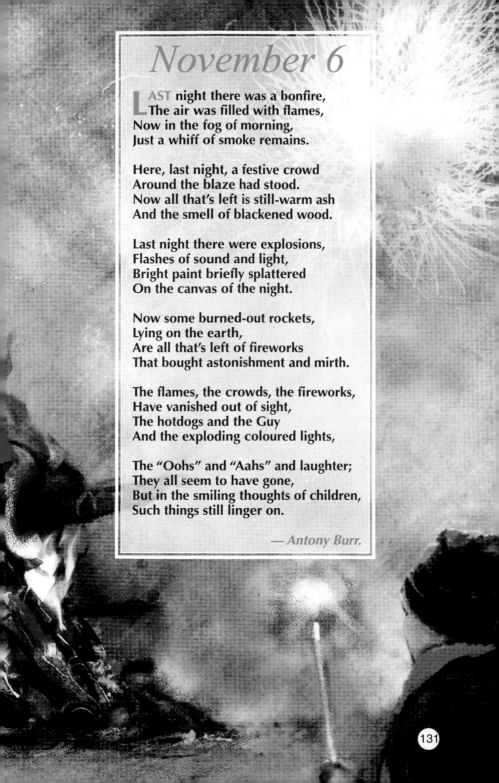

November 6

LAST night there was a bonfire,
The air was filled with flames,
Now in the fog of morning,
Just a whiff of smoke remains.

Here, last night, a festive crowd
Around the blaze had stood.
Now all that's left is still-warm ash
And the smell of blackened wood.

Last night there were explosions,
Flashes of sound and light,
Bright paint briefly splattered
On the canvas of the night.

Now some burned-out rockets,
Lying on the earth,
Are all that's left of fireworks
That bought astonishment and mirth.

The flames, the crowds, the fireworks,
Have vanished out of sight,
The hotdogs and the Guy
And the exploding coloured lights,

The "Oohs" and "Aahs" and laughter;
They all seem to have gone,
But in the smiling thoughts of children,
Such things still linger on.

— *Antony Burr.*

131

Memories

Do you remember frosty ferns
Upon the window pane?
Long icicles that hung from eaves
As winter came again?

Can you recall cold, northern winds
That moaned around the tiles,
And tossed the snowflakes into drifts
Around the old woodpile?

Just think of hearths! Those blazing logs
That made the sparks fly higher!
The children safely home and dry
All sitting round the fire!

— *Maggie Smith.*

Lest We Forget

BIG BEN tolls the eleventh hour
And, in poppy fields, each flower
Symbolises one lost soul
That fate and circumstances stole.
Sacrificed in freedom's name,
With no thought of praise or fame,
So every year we still recall,
And watch, in mind, each soldier fall,
As we parade by cenotaphs
Or gaze at faded photographs.
Rows of ribbons on display,
Reminders of each yesterday.
The times we had, the friendships made,
The highs and lows in retrograde,
And so each year the scene is set,
Lest we forget, lest we forget . . .

— *Brian H. Gent.*

Starlight

I GAZED at the stars in the silent sky
When the earth was calm and still,
And I watched the moon as she sailed aloft
Over the distant hill.
And I wished that this peace could still remain
And last through the coming day,
To calm the world with its stress and strife
And soothe the worries away.

But I knew the darkness would soon be gone
And another dawn appear,
And so I slept in the quietness
Until the day drew near.
And when I awoke, the sun shone out,
A joy for all to see,
But I thanked the stars for the peaceful night
And the hope they gave to me!

— *Iris Hesselden.*

Change Of Scene

I WIND my scarf a little tighter,
Pull my hat about my ears,
Here now comes another winter,
The most severe for many years.
Snowflakes swirling in the lamplight
Quickly covering the ground,
And as the snow lies ever thicker
All is wrapped in muffled sound.
Pointing upwards, blackened branches,
Now bereft of all their leaves,
Vice-like cold grips toes and fingers,
Icicles hang long from eaves.
Smoke is curling up from chimneys
As the oak-logged fires glow,
Woodland creatures hibernating,
Sheltered from the winds that blow,
So now's the time for waiting
For that magic change of scene,
When we will wake one morning
And see a bud turn green . . .

— *Brian H. Gent.*

139

The Magic of Christmas

IT'S not often that a Christmas card is popped through the letterbox right in the middle of summertime, but at that very point in the calendar a few years ago, we received one here at the Manse! The card, wishing us the compliments of the season, was signed by Jack, Eva and Gordon — and we simply hadn't a clue as to whom these good people were!

However, there was a comment written on the back of the card which revealed all. It read, *Bet you're the only ones to receive a Christmas card mid-July, depending on the postal services!*

Let me explain. Friends from south of the border had spent a few days at the Manse during the previous month. When with us, they took some photographs which they said they would send on to us in due course and they used this old Christmas card which they had obviously received the previous Christmas from their friends, Jack, Eva and Gordon, to keep the photographs flat in the post!

However, the words of greeting which were actually printed on the Christmas card by the manufacturer were revealing, too. They read as follows: *May the magic and message of Christmas remain with you*

throughout the coming year.

These words set me thinking. Certainly, the "magic of Christmas" is a common and hackneyed seasonal cliché but it is most definitely real and so impressive, especially if you have the privilege of seeing Christmas through the eyes of a child.

For the young ones, a kind of transformation takes place. Suddenly and amazingly their everyday world is transformed into a fairyland, where sleighbells ring and snowflakes glisten and lights twinkle! And for all of us, our cities, towns and villages throughout the world adopt a carnival air of expectancy with a mysterious yet purposeful bustle of activity.

Not only is Santa in his Grotto — he's everywhere! In our town square he can annually be seen on the back of a lorry in the form of a yuletide DJ hosting a rollicking, reverberating roadside party — all in the interests of local charities, of course!

Life during these days seems full of exciting secrets eager to be told, and presiding over it all is this legendary bearded figure who seems to be able to make magic real, and to make dreams come true! Albeit for a few

Continued on page 142.

By the Rev. Ian W.F. Hamilton

A Country Calendar For ... *Winter*

Thinkstockphotos.

● Bonfire Night, on November 5, with its traditional burning of the "Guy", officially celebrates Guy Fawkes's failed attempt to blow up Parliament in 1605 in the Gunpowder Plot, though the event is probably a conversion of a much older fire rite at the time of year of the Celtic festival, Samhain.

● November 11 has special significance, not just as Armistice Day, but as Martinmas Day – the feast of St Martin, historically a time of celebratory feasting and when farm labourers would seek new posts. The traditional meal of the day would be a meat dish of beef.

Thinkstockphotos.

from the Manse Window

Continued from page 140.

short days in the year magic reigns because, as implied on that Christmas card, Christmas is magic!

That card also spoke of the message of Christmas. Beneath the magic of the season there lies the message. Indeed, the magic is only temporary, whereas the message is eternal. As someone once wrote, "Far greater than the wonder of Jesus's birth is the glory of his life and death and rising!"

The message at the heart of Christmas is surely that God came for

Thinkstockphotos.

> *If there's ice in November that will bear a duck, there'll be nothing after but sludge and muck.*

● Once birch trees have lost their leaves, keep watching for the arrival of woodpeckers – they often become regular visitors because the wood is easy for them to break through, reaching the tasty insects inside!

Thinkstockphotos.

● St Andrew's Day falls on November 30. He is the patron saint of Scotland, and also of Ukraine, Russia, Sicily, Greece, Romania and the Philippines. He was Simon Peter's brother, and both were fishermen to trade.

Thinkstockphotos.

FACT – While November is our eleventh month, it is the ninth of the old Roman year, which began with March.

us in Jesus Christ. He lived for us, he died for us and he rose for us. The advent and the birth of Jesus Christ can never be considered apart from his crucifixion and his resurrection.

Even as Mary and Joseph looked out from the Bethlehem stable into the clear starlit skies above, "the shadow of a Cross arose upon a lonely hill." The wonder of his birth, the glory of his Cross and the triumph of his rising are all part and parcel of the Christmas message.

The heart of the message of God coming down to earth from heaven in the form of that precious baby is that each one of us is precious in the sight of God and that this special child is the

Continued on page 144.

from the Manse Window

Continued from page 143.

way to life for all of God's children. This is the surely the sum and substance of the Christmas message.

However, it also occurred to me that there are two additional "m"s that must be included here, because they are also part and parcel of the sentiments of the season. First of all, in terms of the Christian faith, we must always make room for miracles!

"Glory to God in the highest, and on earth, peace, goodwill toward men," the angel said, accompanied by "a heavenly host of angels."

The mention of angels always evokes an element of the miraculous in our minds. Part of the mystery of the season is that the message of Christmas has stayed alive for us during all seasons for over two thousand years, since the time when that great taxation decree went out from Caesar Augustus.

Part of the miracle is that millions of people of all races and colours throughout the world are annually drawn to kneel in humility and in reverence at the Bethlehem manger, and to sing their simple praise, their humble songs of thanksgiving for the gift of Jesus Christ!

Miraculously, the message has got through that Jesus Christ came to live and ultimately to die for wayward souls, and that he comes again and again, Christmas after Christmas, year after year. As the writer of the lovely carol has so succinctly put it:

"O holy child of Bethlehem descend to us, we pray,

Cast out our sin and enter in, be born in us today."

THERE is a final "m", again not alluded to in that "summer" Christmas card sent to our Manse, but which I would like to feature briefly. I do so because I feel it is so relevant to those of us who have experienced and have been touched and captivated by the magic, the message and the miracle of the season — it is surely the mandate of Christmas.

I have no doubt that, to those of us who have believed in this marvellous and momentous event, a mandate has been squarely given! The mandate given to us is the one given by Jesus himself to his disciples, namely to take the glad tidings, the great joy and the immortal love of Christmas "into all the world" that others may share in the blessing of the incarnation of Jesus Christ.

Those of us who are annually drawn to celebrate this great event "which has come to pass which the Lord has made known to us" are charged with the responsibility of taking the message of Christmas with us wherever we go! To take with us the news, the joy and the love it contains and share it with all those we encounter in our daily lives.

The word "angel" is often translated as "messenger", and surely this is where we come in! As the words of a contemporary hymn encourage us:

"Take us then, Lord, and use us, thy messengers to be;

Our prayers, our gifts, our service we offer here to thee,

That every man and nation may learn what we have heard,

And all the minds of millions shall feed upon thy word."

The final clause printed in our Christmas card that arrived at the Manse in the middle of July expressed the hope that the magic and message of Christmas may remain with us "throughout the coming year."

Although we celebrate the birth of Jesus Christ towards the end of December, there's a very real sense, I finally thought, in which Jesus Christ is born to countless folks right throughout the year!

Wherever and whenever men, women, boys and girls first hear about Jesus and his love for them, in a sense, it's Christmas!

Jesus is born in their hearts and in their lives and what a wonderful day that must be for them! Oh, there are no wise men, no shepherds, no stable, no star, no manger, no gold or frankincense or myrrh, but the sentiments of the greeting ultimately focussed my mind on the thought that for someone, somewhere, any day of any year can be Christmas day! ●

Thinkstockphotos.

146

December Sea

THEY say these are the dead days,
These weeks of dark and chill,
The drained and silent dead days,
When all the world stands still.
Yet if you'd know the winter,
Alive and rich and real,
Then walk beside the ocean
And breathe, and touch, and feel.
And watch the wild waves cresting,
And hear them crash and roar,
And feel the crunch of shingle
That tumbles on the shore.
Embrace the salt wind's bluster
That sets the sand to sing,
And turn your face to sea-spray,
And feel its needle sting.
Just lift your hands, accepting
The gifts the ocean gives,
And as they fill your senses
You'll know that winter lives.

— *Dawn Lawrence.*

Magical Display

WHITE frost lies on the meadows
And mist lies on the hill,
The trees are standing, stark and bare,
The wind is blowing chill.

And yet, last night, the sky was clear,
The clouds have moved away,
Myriad glittering stars appeared —
A magical display!

And though the earth lies still asleep
And ice forms on the lakes,
Reach out to all the shining stars
Until the spring awakes.

— *Iris Hesselden.*

A Mood For Food

I PUT on weight in winter-time,
But that's how things should be,
Everybody does the same —
It isn't only me!
Winter is the time, you see,
To think of comfort food,
And when there's frost and snow outside,
It puts one in the mood.

I think of broth with golden pearls
Of fat — all piping hot;
Of spicy soups and sizzling stews,
All bubbling in a pot.
Potatoes roasting come to mind,
With crispy Yorkshire pud.
And bacon cooked with sausages
That always smells so good.

I think of bottled fruit and jams,
And hot, well-buttered toast;
Of tarts and pies all heated up,
With custard I love most.
I think of porridge thick with cream,
Made just the way I wish;
Of suet pudding steaming hot
With syrup in a dish.

It isn't really time to think
Of losing weight, you see;
Winter comfort just means food!
It isn't only me!

— *Dawn Lawrence.*

Winter Advice

WHEN one's ears are red and fingers are white,
And the wind has a bite like a dog,
Then sensible folk shut their doors for the night,
And are warmed by a blazing log.

When the first snows of winter descend from the sky,
Flakes falling as quiet as a ghost,
Then watch from the window, don't stray outside,
And make platefuls of hot buttered toast.

When the first snows of winter lie on the ground,
The fields look like they're covered in lace,
The world may seem pretty, but don't be deceived,
A warm hearth is a pleasanter place!

When the first snows of winter have gone from the land,
And the air has been warmed by the sun,
Go outside if you must! I prefer it indoors,
There's plenty more winter to come!

— *Antony Burr.*

The Trees

I LOVE the trees in winter,
  When the branches are quite dark,
When all the leaves have fallen
And their shape is plain and stark.
I really love the picture
When their natural form is clear,
When their arms like charcoal etchings
Drawn on the clouds appear.
When the passage of the song-birds
Silhouettes against the sky,
And I can glimpse the owl that lives
Up in a hole on high.
Yet when the winter's over
There's a moment I adore —
To see the trees begin to blush
Back into life once more.

— *Dorothy Morris.*

The Carol Singers

DARK the night and chill the weather,
Icy air and flakes of snow.
In the gold beneath the streetlamp
Carol singers, cheeks aglow,
Stamp their feet against the winter,
Lift their faces to the sky,
Raise their voice in songs of gladness
Sending music soaring high.
Ancient message, newly minted,
Come, rejoice, the carols call,
May this season bless and warm you;
Peace on earth! Goodwill to all!

— Maggie Ingall.

157

Fleeting Moments

WHEN I was young and very small,
With the lamp lit in the hall,
We'd gather round the fire's glow,
My mam and dad and brother Joe.
Oh, what special spells we wove,
Roasting chestnuts on the stove.
Later, when I was a lad,
I'd go fishing with my dad.
Catch or not, we loved the way
That we could spend a tranquil day,
And when the day turned into night
We'd sit and muse by firelight.
Then came those dreadful wartime years,
With all the blood and sweat and tears,
Watching still the fire's flames,
Lit by Blitzkrieg aeroplanes.
But now I'm old, with time to spare
To sit by fire's light and stare,
Remembering those days now gone
As steadfastly the clock ticks on,
Fleeting moments in full measure
Bring firelight memories to treasure.

— *Brian H. Gent.*

from the Manse Window

Perks of the Season

WINTER came down with an iron hand last December. Here in North Yorkshire, the moorland roads were often impassable with huge drifts of snow being swept across by the wind. Farmers in remote dales were cut off for days, and during the worst of the blizzards travellers found themselves trapped in high-standing inns, unable to leave.

The snow and ice brought many a difficulty in its wake. The notorious hill at Sutton Bank, with its gradient of twenty-five per cent, was closed at times and people were unable to get to work in towns such as Thirsk and Northallerton.

Even harder hit were those living in the Pennines and mountainous regions of Scotland. Many were stranded on trunk roads, unable to move until a snow plough came to the rescue. It was a field day for plumbers, with burst pipes, frozen boilers and central heating systems that seized up under the strain of such low temperatures.

I recall two incidents from that bitterly cold time. My wife and I were both involved in the midnight mass at our church, which lay some seven miles away. I was doing the prayers and singing in the choir and she was serving at the altar and administering the chalice or cup of wine.

As evening closed in we watched the heavily falling snow with growing dismay. Nor were the sheets of ice that had formed good news. By eleven o'clock that night it had stopped snowing, but we faced a fourteen-mile round trip on roads that had not been gritted and were barely visible under the coating of snow. Glittering ice showed up in the glare of the headlights.

It was a scary drive and I rarely exceeded twenty miles an hour. Every time the crest of a hill came into view I sat tensely behind the driving wheel wondering whether we would make it or end up with spinning wheels and an abrupt halt.

It was a great relief to arrive home at a quarter to two in the morning safe and sound, and I thanked the angels for watching over us.

The other happening has a humorous side to it.

It was my turn to be chef for the evening meal and I had laid on something rather special. Moussaka, cooked to a recipe from a book we had picked up in Greece, roast potatoes, green beans and fennel. I peered through the glass door of the

Continued on page 162.

By the Rev. David Bryant

A Country Calendar For ... *Winter*

● Advent begins on the fourth Sunday before Christmas, which falls between November 27 and December 3. The name is derived from the Latin word *adventus*, meaning "coming", and the season is concerned with preparation and expectant waiting for Christmas, and the celebration of the nativity of Jesus.

● December 22 marks the winter solstice in the northern hemisphere. Also known as the longest night or shortest day, it marks the date when the sun reaches the tropic of Capricorn.

Thinkstockphotos.

from the Manse Window

Continued from page 161.

oven. Everything was browning nicely and according to plan.

"It'll be ready in half an hour," I called up the stairs to my wife, who was busy making bead necklaces. Famous last words, for at that moment the power went off and the house was plunged into darkness. We gathered together every candle in the house but the meal was completely ruined, so we ended up eating cheese sandwiches and drinking lukewarm tea crouched over a gas fire!

Winter does have another side to it

● The blackthorn tree, with its dark bark and heavenly pure white blossom has been seen as both a good luck and bad luck omen over the years. It is, though, considered to be unlucky to bring it inside the house, unless you live in Hertfordshire, where, if a scorched crown of the plant was hung up inside on New Year's morning, the household would be blessed with good luck that year.

If sun shines through the apple trees upon Christmas Day, When autumn comes, they will a load of fruit display.

Thinkstockphotos.

Thinkstockphotos.

● December 28 is Holy Innocents Day, or Childermas, and is the date when King Herod's tragic killing of all the male babies in Jerusalem is commemorated. In days gone by, before Christmas itself was so focused on children, this was the day for spoiling young ones with treats and parties.

FACT – Originally called "Yule monath" by the Anglo-Saxons because of the custom of burning the Yule log around this time, December's name changed to "Heligh monath", or Holy month, after many converted to Christianity.

— the season is not all grim and forbidding. On the chilliest day of the year, when the car thermometer was reading minus fourteen — a few degrees colder than the North Pole — we drove to Scarborough.

The trees beside the road were completely frozen and every branch and twig was white and glistening, turning it into an enchanted forest. The whole world seemed to be made of ice and it was stunningly beautiful. Both of us agreed that it was one of the most wonderful sights we had ever witnessed.

I remember, too, a number of happy occasions when our grandson came to stay. Being only two, he had never

Continued on page 164.

from the Manse Window

Continued from page 163.

seen snow before so I lifted him up on to the window ledge and held him while he looked out in amazement at all the white flakes floating down from the sky. Later, we took him out into the yard and showed him how to make snowballs and throw them against the garage wall, where they burst.

All the rest of the day he wanted to put on his wellies and play in the snow. He was looking at winter with the wondering eyes of a child. The pavements were transformed, too. The ice was so slippery that few pedestrians were out but that did not put off the youngsters. They were out with toboggans and home-made sledges having the time of their lives.

One morning we woke to find thick ice coating the inside of the bedroom window, despite the central heating having been on. We learned later that it had dropped to minus seventeen during the night, and the ice had traced beautiful patterns on the window glass. I was quite sorry when it melted later!

There were other perks. One evening, as dusk was falling, I went for a walk across the fields, deep snow crunching under foot. Lights from houses at the far side were throwing a gentle orange glow over the scene, turning the landscape into a mysterious world. The sky was clear that night, so I stood staring upwards.

Clearly visible was Orion's Belt, three bright stars in a row, shining in the heavens. I recalled how, in Latin America, people refer to the constellation as the Three Marys, after the three women who went together to the sepulchre of Jesus — Mary, the mother of Jesus, Mary Magdalene and Mary, the mother of James.

On my way back, I passed another incredible sight. Icicles four feet long, and sharp, were hanging like stalactites from the house eaves. In one cottage garden, somebody had built a giant snowman. It had a hat on its head, a carrot nose, cinder eyes, and a striped scarf round its neck. It reminded me of a story-book I had owned when a child. It told of a snowman who came alive and set off on all kinds of adventures once the rest of the world was safely asleep.

THOMAS MERTON, a monk born of New Zealand and American parents, adds yet another dimension to winter. Not only does he glory in the beauty of the season, he sees God in every part of it. He lived from 1915 to 1968, but as a young man and eventually a schoolteacher he had no time for religion. "I believe in nothing," he once said. But that was all to change.

He experienced a conversion and entered the Monastery of Gethsemani in Kentucky. This was the home of Trappist monks known as the Order of Cistercians of the Strict Observance. They lived hard, ascetic lives devoted to prayer, work and sacred reading and they rarely spoke, unless in praise of God.

Thomas Merton felt a growing call to lead a life of complete seclusion after some while and the abbot gave him permission to become a hermit. He moved into a cinder block building in the monastery grounds, hidden away in the woods. Winters in that part of Kentucky are extremely cold and he writes movingly of how he found God during the harsh months in his isolated hut.

One day he goes for a silent walk with a fellow monk. They wander into the woods and amongst the black, leafless trees and in the beautiful silence he has a spiritual encounter.

"Later we separated to pray apart in the thinned pine grove and I could see how simple it is to find God in solitude."

On another occasion he tells of sitting alone looking at the icy, bubbling stream and bare willow trees. In the distance are the blue Kentucky hills, lit by a cobalt sky in which the moon is visible. It is as if he is sitting in the Garden of Eden with Christ. Before going to his hut, he drinks the clear water pouring from a cleft in the mossy rock. He finds himself overflowing with joy. The land, the woods and the stream — all are praising God.

I have a book of daily readings containing excerpts from Thomas Merton and his writings have changed the way I look at winter. I used to dread it as a cold, bleak time, one to be endured until the arrival of spring.

Now I view each day as a gift, a precious time in which to glimpse God's glory. The beauty of the soft, falling snow, the glitter of ice on a pond, a keen wind tearing the moor tops, the trees frozen and white are hints of the presence of God.

Neighbours helping each other to clear drives or start cars, children sledging, youngsters skating and older people sitting comfortably round the fire as the wind moans outside are a reminder of the God who brings joy and comfort.

The star-studded likes of a winter's night, the moors clothed in a blanket of snow and icicles dangling from eaves are full of the grandeur of God. Thomas Merton, in his hermitage in the cold Kentucky hills, saw every moment of winter as an opportunity to praise God, and despite the reputation of the season, I'm inclined to agree with him. ●

Thinkstockphotos.

Spirit Of Christmas

WE have iced the cake,
  Got mince-pies to bake,
The tree hung with baubles,
Coloured streamers to make.

There are carols to sing
To a small baby King,
Friends and family to welcome
As bright gifts they bring.

In the home's warming glow,
While the firelight burns low,
We think of our loved ones
And the days long ago.

And with warm-hearted loving
As the source of our giving,
The spirit of Christmas
Most surely is living.

— *Maggie Smith.*

A New Beginning

I'LL begin life afresh, have another new start,
Live today and look forward, not back;
I'll find time to assess
Blessings which I possess,
Not bemoan all the things that I lack.

How exciting the unknown, the joy it can bring,
If I positively look for the best;
Good intentions in mind,
I solve problems I find,
And let God take care of the rest.

— *Chrissy Greenslade.*

The Coming Year

O^N the last day of December,
As the old year fades away,
Excited people gather
To welcome New Year's Day.

They greet old friends with pleasure,
And talk of folk they've known,
Of all the happy times they've shared
In the days that now have flown.

They share a meal together,
As they've often done before,
And wonder what adventures
The New Year has in store.

And when the midnight hour arrives,
They toast the coming year,
And joining hands their voices raise
A chorus of good cheer.

— *Rosemary Bennett.*

Nature's Promise

WHEN I looked out this morning
Every garden tree was bare.
The sky was grey, and there were signs
Of winter everywhere.

The lawn, which in the summer
Is a pleasant shade of green,
Was shrouded 'neath a snowdrift
So no hint of grass was seen.

And as I watched some feathered snowflakes
Fluttered in the air.
They settled on the frozen ground
And drifted here and there.

My garden was a wilderness;
It made a sombre scene,
Yet, in a tiny spot, I thought
I saw a touch of green.

And in a sheltered corner
Where the snow was thinly spread,
A pretty little snowdrop
Had pushed up its tiny head.

And when I saw this miracle
My heart began to sing,
For this was nature's promise that
Quite soon it would be spring!

— Alice Drury.

"And the light shineth
in darkness; and
the darkness
comprehended it not."
— John 1:5.